The B

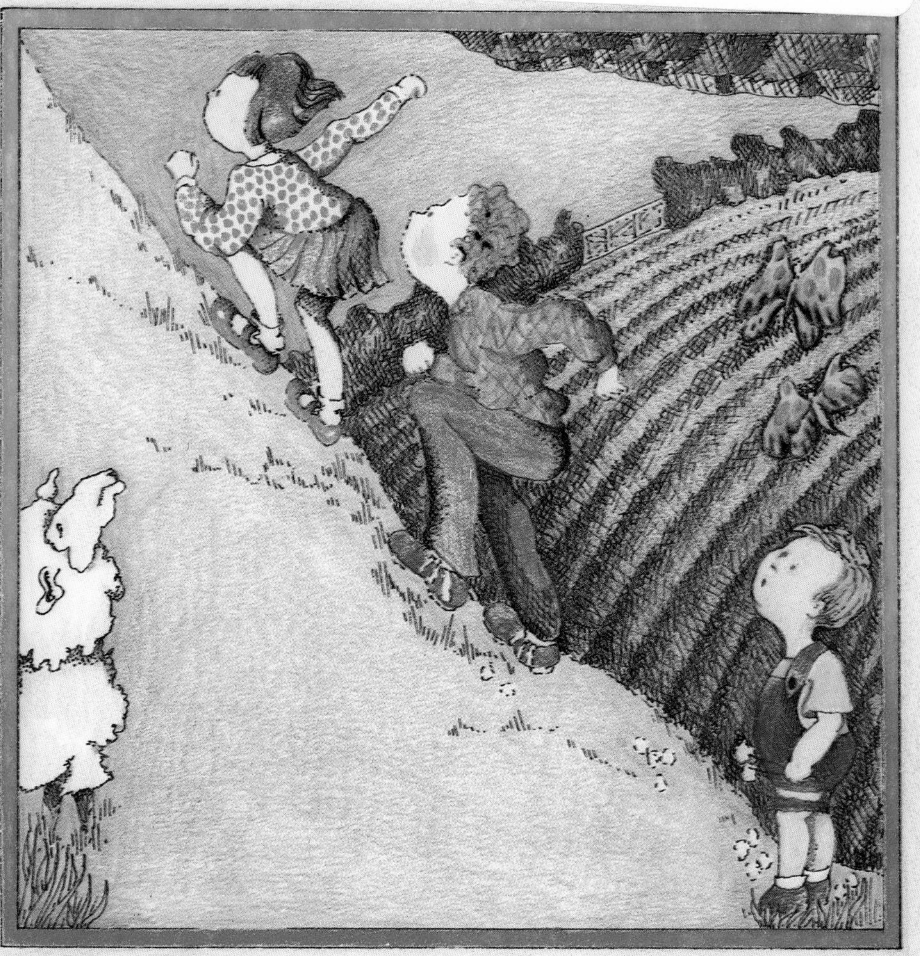

Story by Joy Cowley • Illustrations by Rita Parkinson

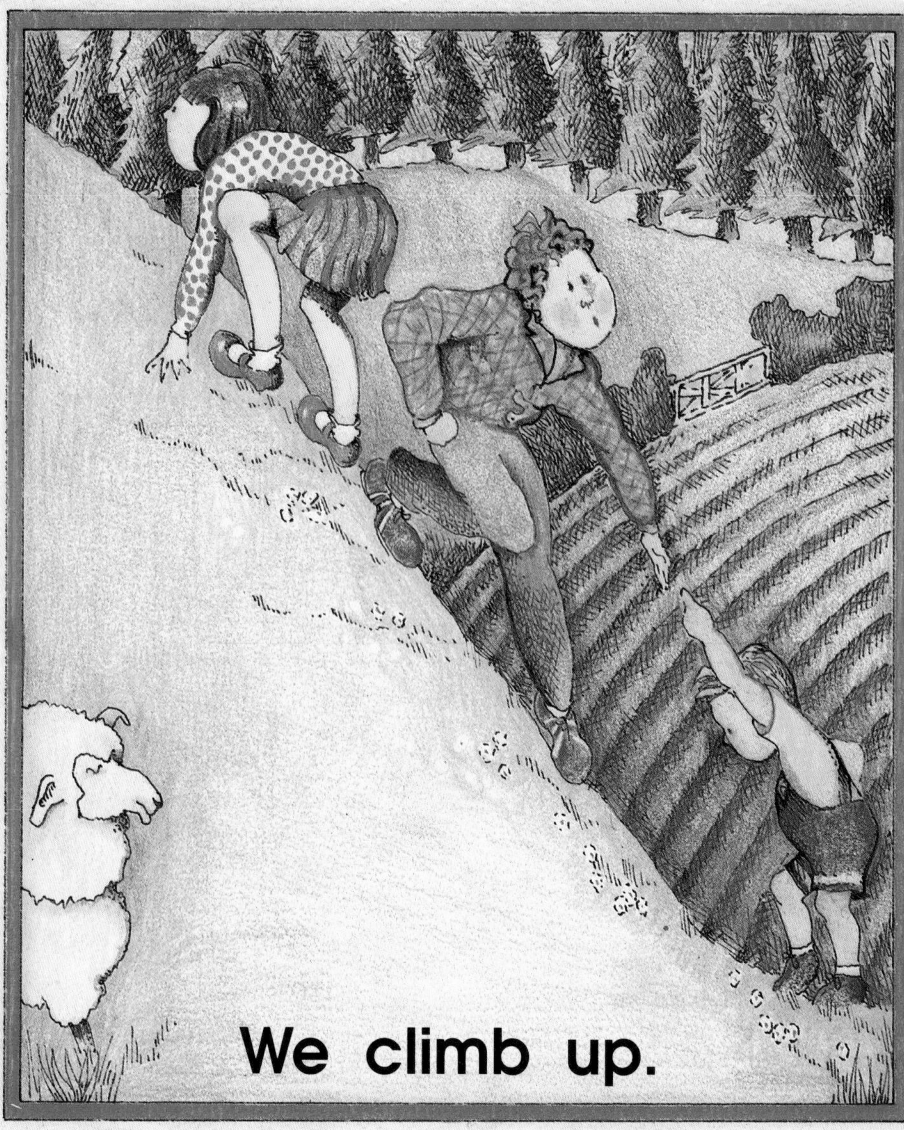

We climb up.

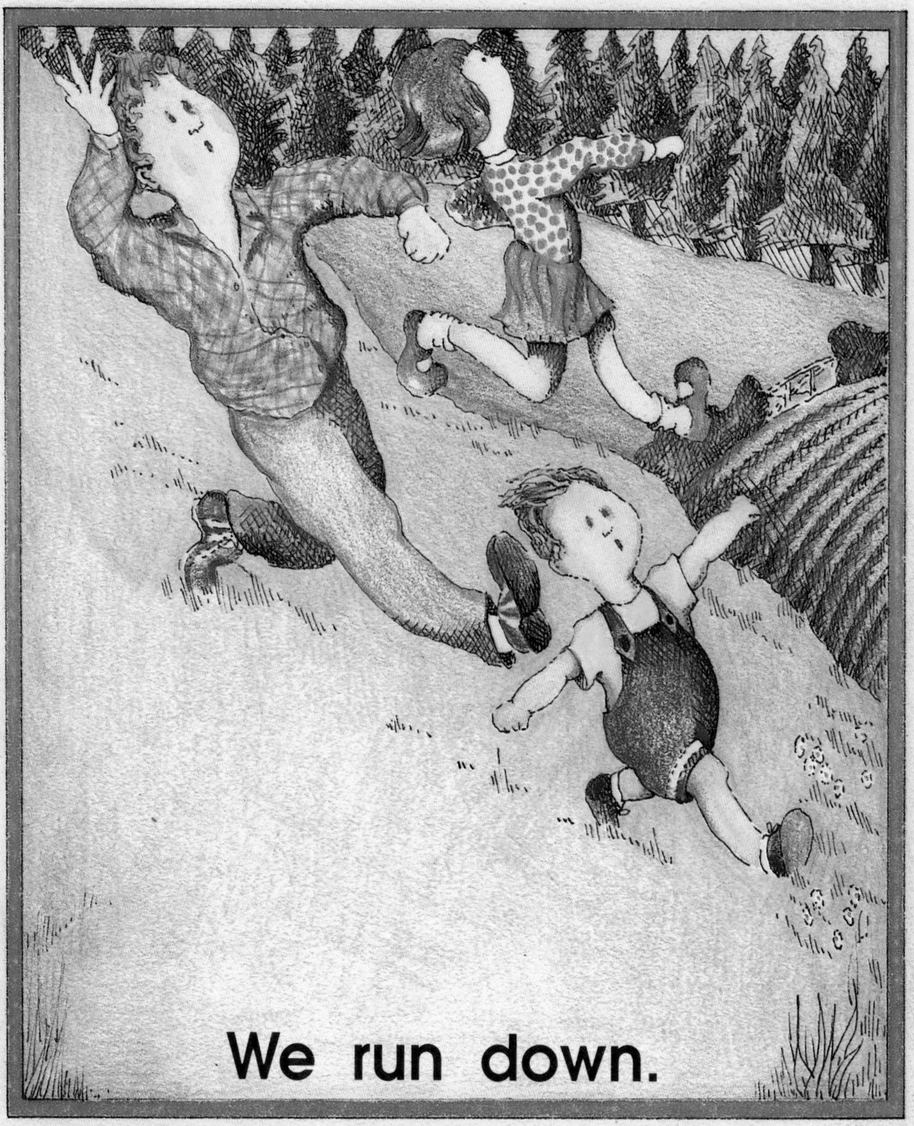

We run down.

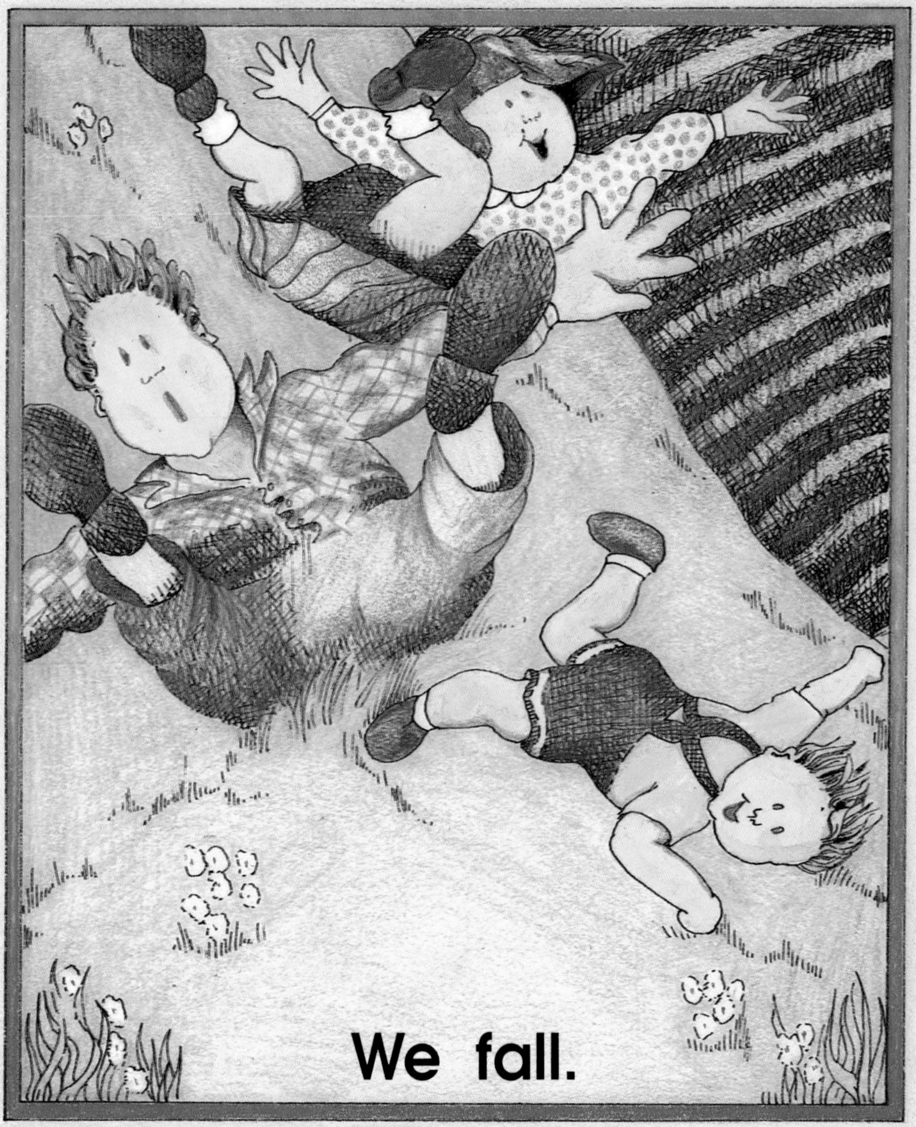

We fall.

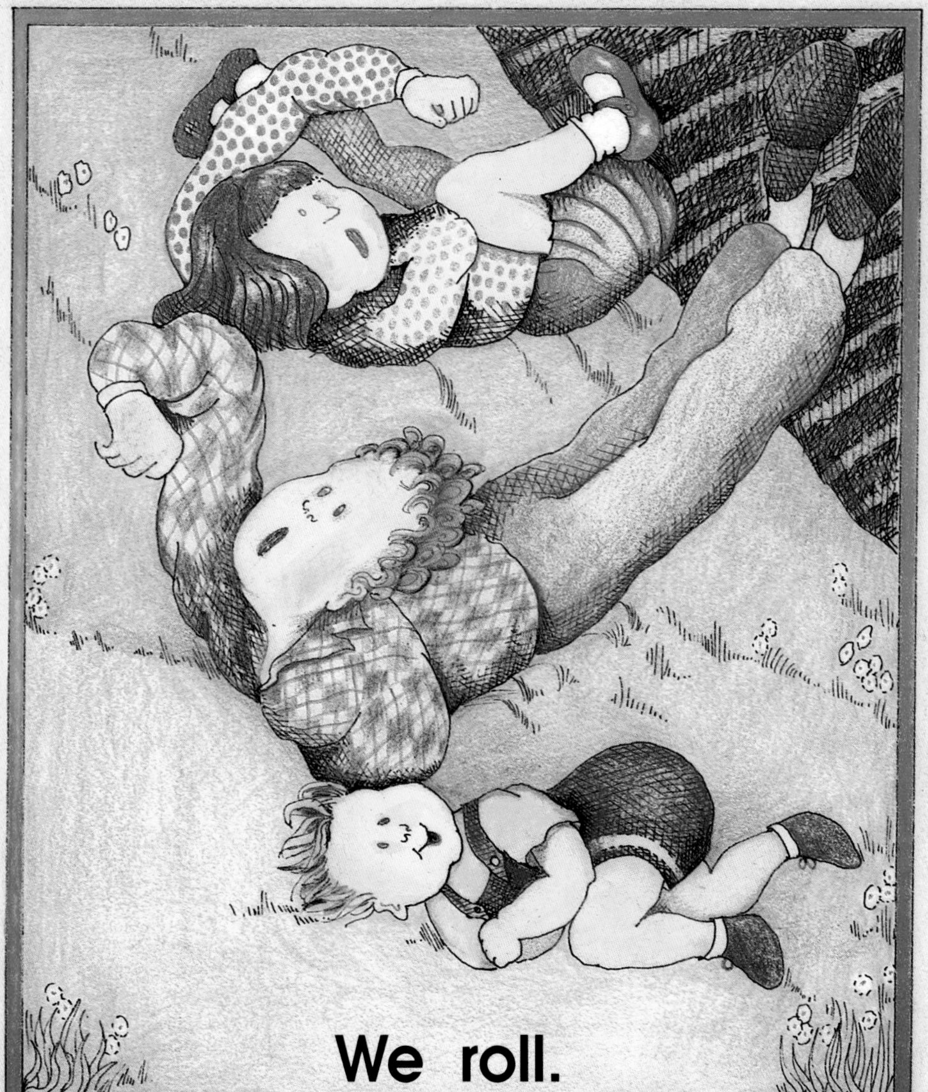

We roll.

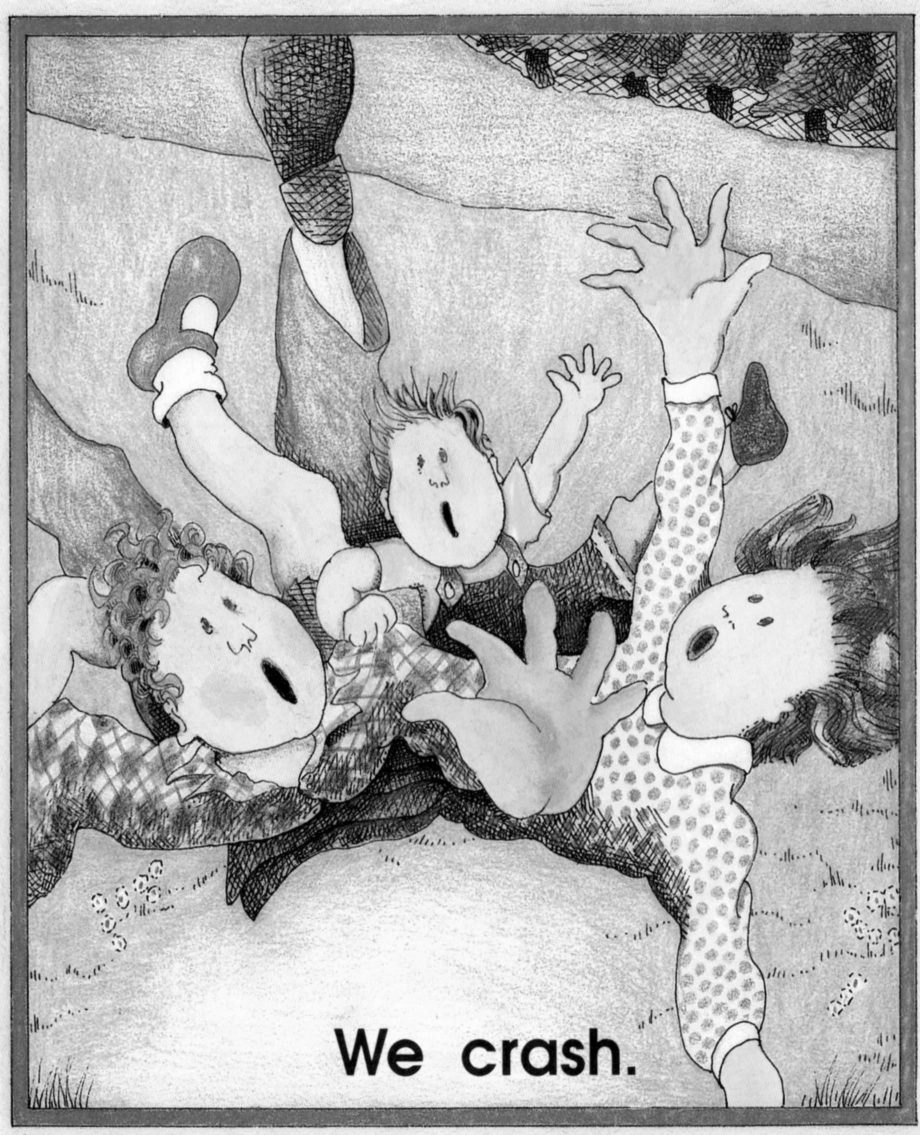
We crash.

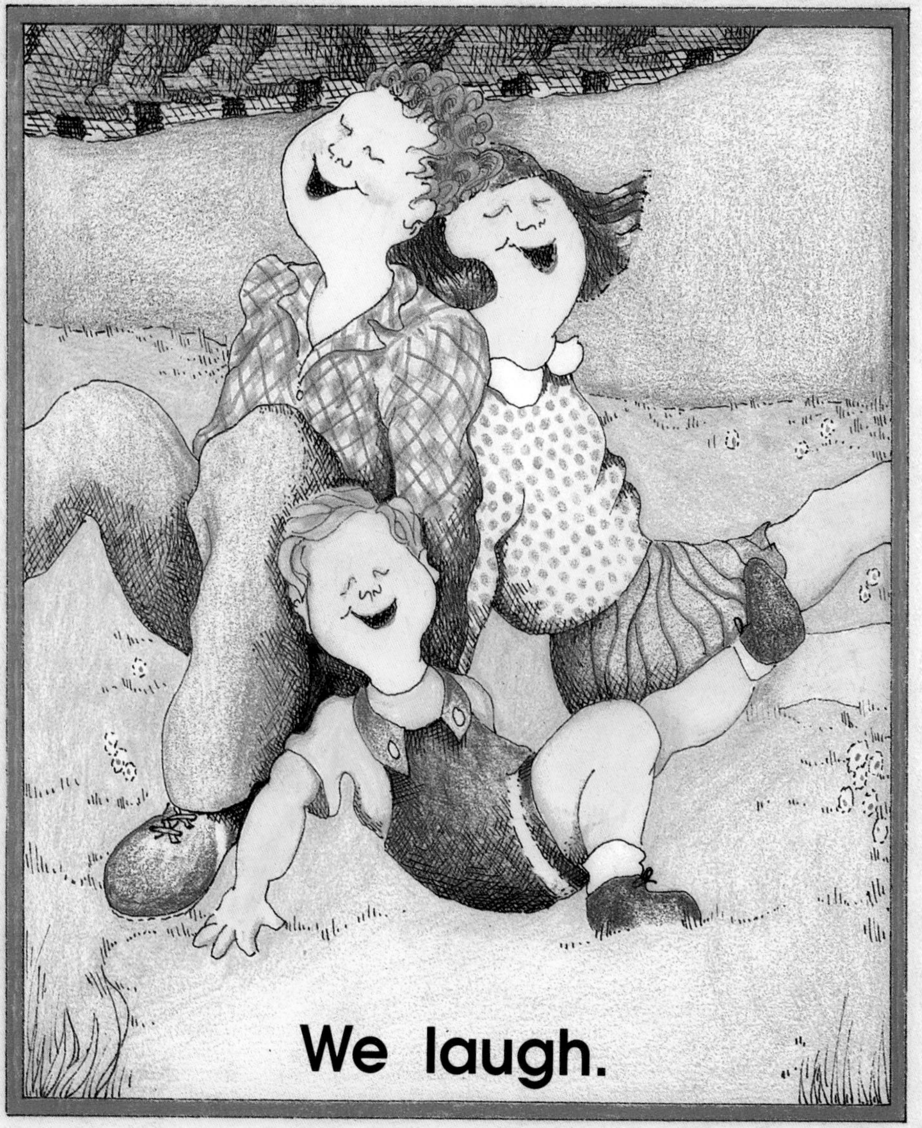

We laugh.

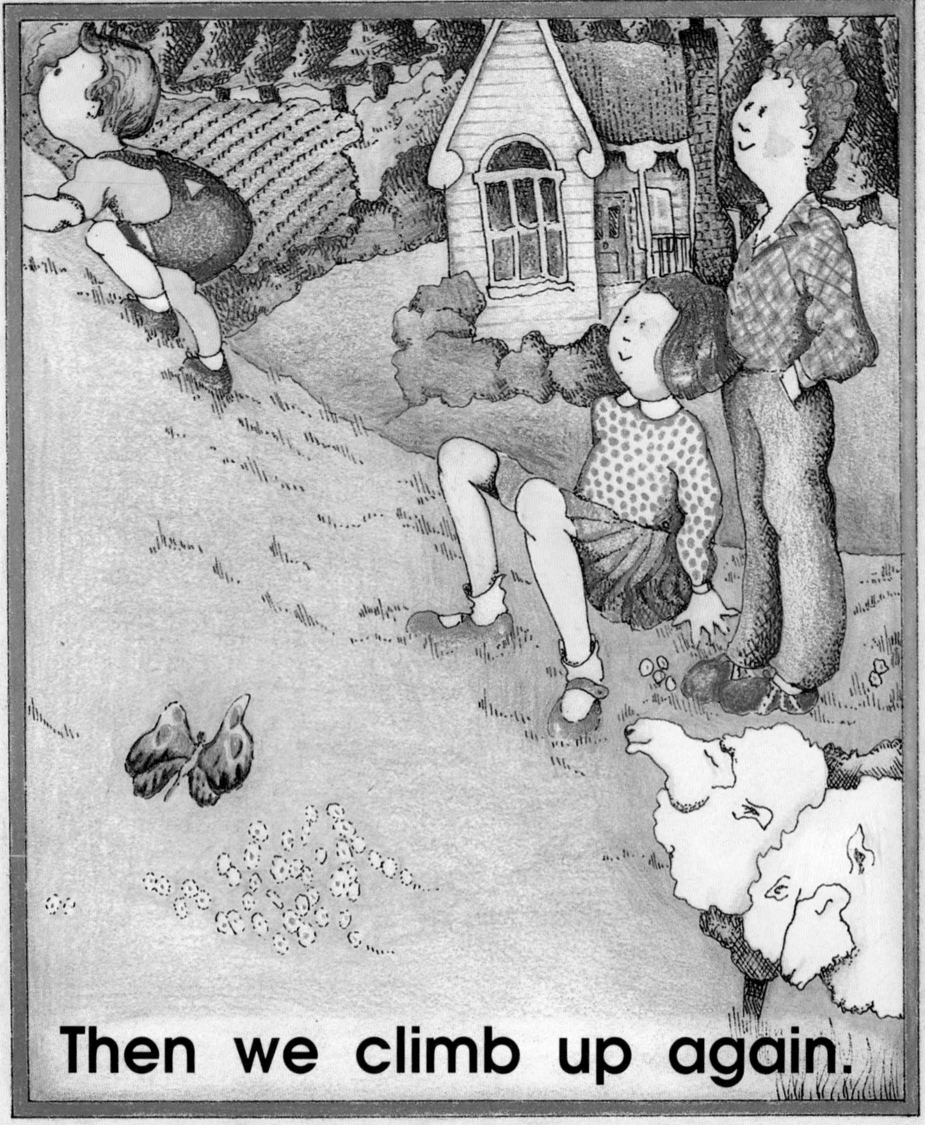

Then we climb up again.